T0353824

HIS EYE IS ON THE SPARROW

A Devotional Inspired by Nature: Volume I

Shirley D. Andrews

WestBow Press books may be ordered through booksellers or by contacting:

WestBow Press
A Division of Thomas Nelson & Zondervan
1663 Liberty Drive
Bloomington, IN 47403
www.westbowpress.com
1 (866) 928-1240

ISBN: 978-1-9736-0667-3 (sc)
ISBN: 978-1-9736-0666-6 (e)

Library of Congress Control Number: 2017916102

Print information available on the last page.

WestBow Press rev. date: 02/02/2018

ACKNOWLEDGMENTS

I extend a special thank you to those who have daily lifted this project to God in prayer and have continually given me words of encouragement. Your prayers and support were essential in taking this devotional from vision to reality. I am especially appreciative of:

Johanna Calabro, loving friend and intercessor, for her faithful prayers and encouragement along this journey of faith, especially her prayers for this first project.

J. Michael Fuller, photographer and praying friend, whose work inspired my writing in each part of this project, from creation in the Book of Genesis to God's plan for eternal life in the Book of Revelation.

Kendra McDonald, my loving granddaughter, who helped me with technology in designing the cover for "His Eye is on the Sparrow."

Carrie Boyer, a loving friend and technology-savvy administrative assistant in the Adirondack District of the United Methodist Church in the Upper New York Conference. I will forever be grateful for her masterful editing of "His Eye is on the Sparrow."

Sharyl Backus, traveling companion and loving friend, who has listened to my problems all along the way from the beginning of this project to publication.

I also want to thank my personal trainer, Nick Galuardi, Rev. Patricia Molik, Rev. Penny Brink and Rev. David Martin, for taking the time to read and endorse my first devotionals. Your guidance and support has blessed me and encouraged me to keep moving forward in ministry.

Shirley Andrews
John 10:9-10

PART

1

Lord God, our Creator and
His Creation on Earth

"In the beginning God created the heavens and the earth. Now the earth was formless and empty, darkness was over the surface of the deep, and the Spirit of God was hovering over the waters. And God said, 'Let there be light,' and there was light. God saw that the light was good, and He separated the light from the darkness. God called the light 'day' and the darkness He called 'night.' And there was evening, and there was morning - the first day.

"And God said, 'Let the water teem with living creatures, and let the birds fly above the earth across the expanse of the sky.' So God created the great creatures of the sea, and every living and moving thing with which the water teems, according to their kinds, and every winged bird according to its kind. And God saw that it was good."

Genesis 1:1-5, 20-21

This devotional presents a variety of small and large land birds and small and large waterfowl. Volume II also includes a few animals from wilderness places. These photos have been taken by a portrait photographer who rarely leaves home without his camera and gear. Most of these photos have been taken in New Mexico, New Jersey, Florida, British Columbia, Wyoming, Montana, Long Island, NY, his backyard in Duanesburg, NY, and other remote places. We have been praying that these devotionals will be a delight to the eye, mind and heart of each of our readers. Preparing these devotionals will be worth it all if God gets the glory.

Whether you are a nature lover, birder, photographer, devotional collector, God lover or God beginner, we hope you will experience God's presence on every page as you meditate on His word and His miraculous creation. May you fall in love with God all over again every time you reopen or turn a page in "His Eye is on the Sparrow." Whether you read or sing through the hymns, they are meant to help enhance your devotional time and connect you with God's heart through His Spirit. As you sing, not only are the birds singing with you, but so is God!

"The Lord your God is with you, He is mighty to save. He will take great delight in you, He will quiet you with His love, He will rejoice over you with singing."

Zephaniah 3:17

When reading, stop and listen to God; tell Him you love Him, and then pray in faith, believing for the desires of your heart. Remember to align your heart with the heart of God and pray God's word back to Him. When possible end each prayer with, "in Jesus' name," Amen.

"Delight yourself in the Lord and He will give you the desires of your heart." Psalm 37:4

Amazing Grace

1. A - maz - ing grace! How sweet the sound that
2. 'Twas grace that taught my heart to fear, and
3. Through man - y dan - gers, toils, and snares, I
4. The Lord has prom - ised good to me, his
5. Yea, when this flesh and heart shall fail, and
6. When we've been there ten thou - sand years, bright

saved a wretch like me! I once was lost, but
grace my fears re - lieved; how pre - cious did that
have al - read - y come; 'tis grace hath brought me
word my hope se - cures; he will my shield and
mor - tal life shall cease, I shall pos - sess, with -
shin - ing as the sun, we've no less days to

now am found; was blind, but now I see.
grace ap - pear the hour I first be - lieved.
safe thus far, and grace will lead me home.
por - tion be, as long as life en - dures.
in the veil, a life of joy and peace.
sing God's praise than when we'd first be - gun.

Cherokee
OOH NAY THLA NAH, HEE OO WAY GEE.'
E GAH GWOO YAH HAY EE.
NAW GWOO JOE SAH, WE YOU LOW SAY,
E GAH GWOO YAH HO NAH.

Navajo
NIZHÓNÍGO JOOBA' DITTS' A'
YISDÁSHÍÍTÍNÍGÍÍ,
LAH YÓÓÍÍYÁ, K'AD SHÉNÁHOOSDZIN,
DOO EESH'ÍÍ DA ŃT'ÉÉ.

Kiowa
DAW K'EE DA HA DAWTSAHY HE TSOW'HAW
DAW K'EE DA HA DAWTSAHY HEE.
BAY DAWTSAHY TAW, GAW AYM OW THAH T'AW,
DAW K'EE DA HA DAWTSAHY H'EE.

Creek
PO YA FEK CHA HE THLAT AH TET
AH NON AH CHA PA KAS
CHA FEE KEE O FUNNAN LA KUS
UM E HA TA LA YUS.

Choctaw
SHILOMBISH HOLITOPA MA!
ISHMMINTI PULLA CHA
HATAK ILBUSHA PIA HA
IS PI YUKPALASHKE.

WORDS: John Newton, 1779; st. 6 anon.; phonetic transcription Cherokee, Kiowa,   AMAZING GRACE
  Creek, Choctaw as sung in Oklahoma Indian Missionary Conference; Navajo phonetic   CM
  transcription by Albert Tsosi (1 Chr. 17:16-17)
MUSIC: 19th cent. USA melody; harm. by Edwin O. Excell, 1900

2

GRACE

2145   I've Got Peace Like a River

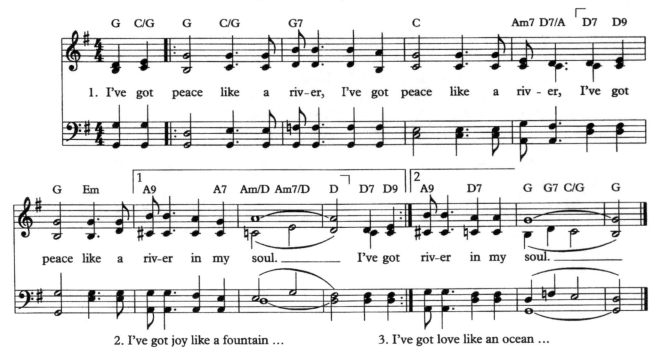

2. I've got joy like a fountain ...

3. I've got love like an ocean ...

Congregation: Unison or parts

WORDS: African American spiritual
MUSIC: African American spiritual

PEACE LIKE A RIVER
77.11 D

2146   His Eye Is on the Sparrow

Congregation: Unison; unison or parts on refrain

WORDS: Civilla Martin (Luke 12:6-7; John 14:1)
MUSIC: Charles H. Gabriel

SPARROW
Irregular with Refrain

The male song sparrow has been gifted by God to sing as many as 20 different melodies on any given spring morning. As evening approaches, he may have improvised as many as 900-plus variations on his basic theme. This musical gift of serenading with such variety and passion wins the heart of his mate and then courtship begins. After all their duet singing, she lays 3 to 6 eggs and incubates them for 12 to 15 days. An inspired singer as well, she gets them singing and ready to fill the world with music in about 10 days, as one by one they leave the comforts of their own recital hall. They become virtuosos like mom and dad as they make their way from one forest concert hall to another, glorifying God and bringing joy to all who are listening. The male's four-note basic theme has been described as very similar to the opening theme in Beethoven's "Fifth Symphony." Then off he goes with many, many variations sung very loudly and very clearly to keep danger far away from the growing choir under conductor mom. She conducts with a baton of love and joy and the youngsters create new compositions as they learn to be outstanding musicians. By fall, this sibling choir has matured into accomplished solo performers who continue in the same traditions of mom and dad. This is nothing short of stunning, miraculous and humbling for some of us less-talented musicians.

"Are not two sparrows sold for a penny? Yet not one of them will fall to the ground apart from the will of your Father. And even the very hairs of your head are all numbered. So don't be afraid; you are worth more than many sparrows."

Matthew 10:29-31

As we read about all the positive qualities of the song sparrows and God's plan for them, we must stop and worship Him, our Creator. We are so much more valuable to God than we realize, and so much more gifted to do His work here on earth than the sparrows. Can we take a moment to marvel at their obedience? Yes, their obedience is a God-given instinct and, yes, we have been given free will. How can we work on surrender and obedience in the days ahead? Let's always take time to listen to God's still, small voice as we pray and as we read His word daily. Why? Because He loves His sparrows, but how much more does He love you? Can you give God first place in your day? Show your obedience by praying with a sincere heart.

Prayer: Lord God, Creator of all life, this is the first day of the rest of my life. I need you more than ever! I am beginning to realize how marvelously you have created me and I do want to know your future plans for me. Help me to grow spiritually as I read through and absorb these devotional pages. Give me Holy-Spirit power to apply the word of God to my life and to share my progress with others who need to hear my testimony. Show me, Lord, where I am going wrong and where the next right path leads. I confess that I often want what I want. Forgive me and restore your closeness to me. I love you, Lord, because I know that you first loved me, in Jesus' name, Amen.

This little 4- to 5-inches of utter sweetness, the chickadee, can delight the heart of the very youngest to the elderly. They travel in flocks of 8 to 12 and have been known to land on an open palm offering peanuts. It tickles a little, but holding your hand very still will allow the feast to continue until the supply is gone. If the whole flock catches on, you may eventually be overcome by the enthusiasm of these petite backyard friends. Secret: Have plenty of snacks to go around!

"Satisfy us in the morning with your unfailing love, that we may sing for joy and be glad all our days."

Psalm 90:14

Maybe you have a habit of experiencing God's unfailing love with every new day. If so, then you have been blessed as you look on this precious little bird. You have probably taken time to meditate on this scripture and maybe prayed it back to God with gratitude in your heart. Then you took time to listen to God's voice for He has so much to say to all of us. That is when you heard Him say, "My love never fails, I will never stop loving you, just as I have never stopped loving my chickadees and all of my creation!"

Others of us may be in a more common place of hustle and bustle today, checking off the list of "what I need to get done today." We find ourselves in this place all too often. We vow to make changes to spend more time with God, but many days He does not get first place, second place or third. It is true that He does not need you, but do you need to hear from Him? Do you need His healing power and love?

Prayer: Lord God, as you provide insects, seeds and berries for the chickadees, I ask you to bring me into your holy presence that I might "taste and see that the Lord is good." Let me linger in your embrace and open my heart to what your plan is for this new day. As I experience your unfailing love, my heart will sing for joy and my mind will be renewed. Teach me more about who you are and what your plans are for the next 24 hours. Lord, I can't wait to see what you and I are going to do together today, in Jesus' name, Amen.

BALTIMORE ORIOLE
Duanesburg, NY

Icterus galbula

Fairly common

The vivid colors on this oriole are the inspiration for his name. In the 17th Century, Lord Baltimore and his British family were identified with these same colors on their coat-of-arms. Baltimore, the largest city in Maryland, is also the home of the professional baseball team, the Baltimore Orioles. The female builds the nest alone and the pair, male and female, is often heard singing a duet. The longest recorded lifespan for a wild bird is 11 years, 7 months, with captive orioles living up to 14 years. Does this mean that the oriole is more favored by God than other birds?

"The heavens declare the glory of God; the skies proclaim the work of His hands. Day after day they pour forth speech, night after night they display knowledge."

Psalm 19:1-2

All of God's Creation has been created to bring Him glory. No one bird, animal or person is more significant than another. God loves all of His creation with unfailing and unconditional love. However, the human race, ever since the Garden of Eden, has been born in sin, needing a Savior! Day by day the bird songs bring glory to God. Each warmed egg that gives birth to a new bird is a glorious sight in God's eyes. Night after night, mom and dad protect the young so they can grow, learn to fly and start new nests of their own. What a joy to God's ears when the oriole mates sing a duet in close harmony. The bird world has instinctive habits that glorify God. What old or new habit do you have and enjoy because it brings glory to God? Free will has given us a choice between good and evil. What habit do you want to eliminate because it doesn't glorify our Lord? Talk to Him about it and ask for help. He is listening, and wants you to listen for His answer that will be filled with His unconditional love and forgiveness. Your day will be filled with His peace. There is no freedom here on earth that compares to the God-given freedom from sin and death! Tell others about your grace-filled miracle from our Holy God.

Prayer: Lord God, what a beautiful creation you have given me to enjoy and care for. Help me to follow you so closely that I never miss a bird's song, a new nest or a family being fed by mom and pop. I will stop and give thanks for the gift of my life at birth and the gift of new life at my second birth. Come, Holy Spirit, lead me into new habits that continually glorify you and show others the unconditional love of Jesus Christ, my Lord and Savior. Open up a way for my obedience with new boldness to testify to the lost about the saving power of God and what He has done for me, in Jesus' name, Amen.

Agreeing with the description that this very young bluebird is handsome is a no-brainer! Notice how fluffy his topnotch feathers appear. His father's top feathers are much flatter and less attractive. This 5- to 7-inch beauty looks so healthy and ready to take on the world. His coloring is glorious: white belly, orange breast, capped all over in royal blue with brown wingtips. He has a very human side when he is hungry. He loves it when he finds peanut butter inside his bluebird house or in a backyard feeder. You may already know that he is a very shy bird, but more importantly, the truth is, he is becoming less and less available due to predator birds who steal nesting places from him. Soon we may no longer hear his low, murmuring and lovely song.

"The eyes of all look to you, and you give them their food at the proper time. You open your hand and satisfy the desires of every living thing. The Lord is righteous in all His ways and loving toward all He has made."

Psalm 145:15-17

Having our nesting place suddenly taken from us unjustly is cause for some discomfort or even anger toward the guilty party. But some things are not easy to prove, even when we know who has victimized us. And there is always the fact that some will not believe the truth unless it can be defended with strong evidence. Does God care when these unwanted situations happen to us? YES, He does! As Psalm 145 promises, if we look to God He will be the supply source for whatever we need. He has the solution for these problems. Because He is righteous in all His ways, we must wait for His answer. But waiting is not always easy! He is a just God, and loving toward everything He has made including you, His beloved child, and the bluebirds.

Prayer: Lord God, because you are righteous in all your ways and loving toward all you have made, I choose today to fix my eyes on you, Jesus, the Author and Finisher of my faith. Who for the joy set before you, endured the cross, scorned its shame and you are now seated at the right of the throne of God. Teach me patience as I wait for your solutions to fix my problems. Teach me to show love toward my enemies, especially the ones who steal my joy or hurt me. I know you want me to bless my enemies. Show me how to love them like you love them. I know it will be hard to do, but I will try in Jesus' name, Amen.

Easily recognizable are the bright, mostly yellow, small and fluffy friends in our backyard and patio. Look for their nest on a rainy day and you may find mom covering the whole thing with her wingspan. She resembles a colorful umbrella over her nest. She protects her young from rain and from water filling the nest. Goldfinches fly in flocks and rarely stop singing with sweet twitterings of "Just look at me!" "Just look at me!" Mom and pop chew and predigest the seeds after removing the shells. When this food process is over, they regurgitate it and separate it into small portions for the hungry young. Dropping it slowly into their wide-open beaks, they may sing some more as if offering a prayer of thanks to God for this delicious meal.

"Consider it pure joy, my brothers, whenever you face trials of many kinds, because you know that the testing of your faith develops perseverance. Perseverance must finish its work so that you may be mature and complete, not lacking anything. If any of you lacks wisdom, he should ask God, who gives generously to all without finding fault, and it will be given to him."

James 1:2-5

As disgusting as this bird-feeding process sounds to us humans, how efficiently God has provided wisdom as instinct in the mom and pop goldfinch. Some of us have had to go to a pediatrician to get answers for our newborn when feeding became a serious concern. Small tummies, allergies, colic and cramps are not new to families with a baby, but they have caused worry, frustration and yes, tears, when we can't find a solution in the middle of a long night! Have you ever needed wisdom during childrearing? Or during job hunting? Or buying a used car?

Prayer: Lord God, Creator of all families, grant me your wisdom to persevere in tough times when answers do not come easily. Help me to remember that you have made a way for me to hear your voice, to know your will and to receive your love in the answer to my prayers. I confess that I am far from being mature and complete. Thank you, Lord, for your patience. Come, Holy Spirit, and fill me with faith, love and more trust than ever before, in Jesus' name, Amen.

There it is again: that noisy and scrappy bullying sound on the front porch. After rushing to the dining room window, streaks of beautiful blue, some white and a tiny bit of black hover for just a moment in time. The black ribbon forms an exquisite necklace around his throat. His grayish white belly is in stark contrast to his proud chest. At the sound of the piercing "jeeah," all gentler forms of feathered bodies scatter in a flurry, as if getting away from grave trouble. This very bold, showy intruder has managed to be left alone on the porch with nearly a full feeder all to himself. He has more than he wanted, but no one to share it with.

"But as for me, my feet had almost slipped; I had nearly lost my foothold. For I envied the arrogant when I saw the prosperity of the wicked. Therefore pride is their necklace; they clothe themselves with violence. From their calloused hearts comes iniquity; the evil conceits of their minds know no limits."

Psalm 73:2-3, 6-7

Let's take a short walk back to a time when we were being swayed to and fro by a situation or circumstance, badgered by a friend, scolded by a parent or perhaps disciplined by a boss. We were reminded of some old sayings like: "I feel like I'm between a rock and a hard place" or "I can't see the forest for the trees!" We were feeling misunderstood, violated, confused or maybe so hurt that the pain continues to this day. Are those feelings still haunting us; are we still searching for why that had to happen? Even if our foot slipped and we lost our foothold, God has made a way to these scriptures because He loves us and cares about us. If we have unforgiveness toward ourselves or some other person, then today is a great time to fix it.

"Jesus said, 'If we confess our sins, He is faithful and just and will forgive us our sins and purify us from all unrighteousness.'"

1 John 1:9

Prayer: Lord God, Healer of self-inflicted wounds and the hurt and pain inflicted by others, I confess the sin of unforgiveness and choose to forgive myself and others I name now .... I am beginning to understand that you care about every aspect of my life and I am receiving your love and healing. I will continue to trust you and come to you with all my problems, for Jesus' sake and to glorify His Kingdom, Amen.

This dabbling male duck has diving limitations but still manages to eat without going under water. He is very restless and is always ready to warn the crowd of redheads and canvasbacks when danger is near. So they depend on each other for survival. The redheads and canvasbacks dive very deep down to the celery beds, while "Weggie" waits nearby for the next meal as a watchman on the water. When they surface, he grabs celery right out of their mouths and they comply. They share very willingly because they need "Weggie" to always be watching for danger. His gift is awareness, loud quacking and speed. Their gift is diving for celery and sharing it. What an amazing Creator/Provider we worship!

"Love must be sincere. Hate what is evil; cling to what is good. Be devoted to one another in brotherly love. Honor one another above yourselves. Share with God's people who are in need. Practice hospitality."

Romans 12:9-10, 13

The American wigeon has found his ministry and his gift. His friends who are different in looks and habits are devoted to him and he to them. They need each other's giftedness given to them by God. They need each other for survival. Take a few moments to listen to God's message to you about how you fit into the Body of Christ where He has planted you. This is a picture in nature of what God's plan is for the Body of Christ, the Church. What is God asking of you today?

Sincere love is agape love. Jesus Christ demonstrated agape love on the cross when He was crucified to pay our sin debt in full. Agape love is unconditional love, forgiving love, unique devotion overflowing with amazing grace, never proud or boastful, but full of the humility of our Lord. This is a high calling, but we will never be truly happy until people see only Jesus when they see us.

Prayer: Come, Holy Spirit, and fill me so I can be more like Jesus today than yesterday. I will trust in my Lord and practice sincere love, forgiving each and everyone near and far. Show me today, Lord, who needs my listening ear, my encouragement, my prayers, my support and my unconditional love. Who needs to see you, Lord? In the holy name of Jesus, Amen.

Viewing a purple sandpiper in the summer months is very rare unless you are traveling in the stony Arctic tundra. You can find them there on their breeding turf. When that process is over, you can find them on the rocky shores and inlets of the Northern Atlantic. They hunt by pulling crustaceans, mollusks and algae from the cliffs and tearing apart wet seaweed for small mussels and clams. They even like to float out to sea on the seaweed. But the part that is a little hard to believe is that those mussels and clams go down their throat shells and all! When "Hurricane Sandy" shifted the sandy beaches, crews came and built large stonebreakers to hold the sand in place. When this happened, the purple, rock-loving sandpipers extended their winter range nearly as far south as Georgia. This may help to increase them in numbers in the future, and they could become common instead of uncommon. Surprisingly, the male tends to do most, if not all, of the incubating and tending the nest after the young are hatched. This brings new meaning to "stay-at-home dad!"

"But the Lord said to Samuel, 'Do not consider his appearance or his height, for I have rejected him. The Lord does not look at the things man looks at. Man looks at the outward appearance, but the Lord looks at the heart.'"

1 Samuel 16:7

It doesn't matter if you are dad, the caregiver, or mom, the caregiver, or the nanny, or the daycare person attending our/God's children, your love for children and knowing how to give excellent care is what matters. We, as parents, must hire the very best caregivers that God has to offer if we are a breadwinner of the family and cannot be home on most days. Those who speak with loving words, soft and tender voices, taking time to meet the needs of training, reading, loving and listening are very important to care for our family. God is always looking on our hearts to see if we are representing His unconditional love to all those around us. It is always an area that we can grow better at day by day. How are you doing in this area, mom, dad, caregiver, friend? Ask God to change your attitude and/or your heart when you know that you are falling short of the mark that God has set before you.

Prayer: Lord God, Caretaker of my family, my Shelter in the storm, my Constant Companion, my Best Friend, speak to me about my heart condition as I read, listen, share, love and play with family, friends and co-workers. I want everyone to see Jesus in me and to know His love and His ability to take care of us as we look after our families. Lord, I know that you never leave me or forsake me. I will come to you when making the decisions about caring for my family while I am away at work, in Jesus' name, Amen.

This woodpecker is a hole-digger who finds insects and wood-boring beetles down deep inside the tree bark and wood. If you've ever heard a hole being dug, you will remember how loud and repetitive it sounded. To screen his lungs from the wood dust, God gave him a small mask on his nostrils. And to prevent brain damage from all the drilling with his bill, God gave him a thick skull. But his most notable body part is his unbelievably long, hard tongue for spearing beetles and grasshoppers. His tongue also has the advantage of gluey saliva for lapping up ants. He is very unpopular in the state of Florida. Can you guess why? It's because he loves orange juice! Drilling holes in oranges is frowned upon, but he gets away with it when no one is looking. This reminds us that God has a sense of humor. God is very pleased with His red-bellied woodpecker, and very pleased with you as well.

"How precious to me are your thoughts, O God! How vast is the sum of them! Were I to count them, they would outnumber the grains of sand. When I awake, I am still with you."

Psalm 139:17-18

Even the red-bellied woodpecker is in God's thoughts. But more importantly, this scripture reminds us that we are always on God's mind. He is always here and waiting for our intimate conversation with Him. What do you want Him to hear from you today? Remember, we do not look or act like a woodpecker, but instead we are created in the image of God. How does that make you feel? Now is a good time to tell Him all about it.

Prayer: Lord God, I am fearfully and wonderfully made. In your image you created even me. You have given me precious thoughts about creation, and now I realize how important I am in your plan. In your presence is the fullness of joy! You are there when I rise and you are there when I sleep. Keep my thoughts pure and my path straight for the rest of my journey. I love You, Lord, much more than all the grains of sand that you have made, in Jesus' name, Amen.

The ruddy turnstones like rocky, stony shores. They get their name from their main activity of inserting their short, pointed bills under stones and flipping them with their strong, neck muscles. If an object, like a dead fish, is heavy or stuck, they form a team and together overturn the fish and share a meal. They also help each other roll up mats of seaweed to see if there are any goodies underneath. They go after unattended and undefended nests that may have eggs. They will peck the egg to get at its contents. During spring migration, they especially dig for horseshoe crab eggs. "Ruddy" is a predator, but the egg-owners just stand by and watch without objection. Another favorite meal is sandwich bread and french fries left on the sand by the summer tourists. The ruddy turnstones are monogamous and the pairs stay together for more than one season. Several pairs may nest close together. Sounds like a faith community to me.

"Some wandered in desert wastelands, finding no way to a city where they could settle. They were hungry and thirsty, and their lives ebbed away. Then they cried out to the Lord in their trouble, and He delivered them from their distress. For He satisfies the thirsty and fills the hungry with good things."

Psalm 107:4-6, 9

The ruddy turnstones aren't the only wandering, hungry and thirsty creatures in God's creation. Since the beginning of time, people have been lost and searching for daily provisions and Godly purpose. If you have been living life unsure of your purpose, you have come to the right place. God, our Creator, has an individual purpose for each of His children. If you have only read prayers and never spoken your own words to Jesus, today would be a great day to start that personal relationship. He is waiting with unconditional love and grace. He will speak into your heart with the message of purpose. You will need to be still and let Him speak. We have to go to Him for His answers for each of us individually. You will want to go to Him often because you will be very thirsty for more of Jesus. His love, kindness, patience and plans are contagious, and only He can satisfy your longings.

Prayer: Lord God, I am one of those wanderers who have avoided talking to you personally for a long time. I am thirsty for more than what I have experienced so far. I want a strong, personal relationship with you. Forgive me for taking so long to get to this place of surrender. I want to learn what pleases you in worship, in prayer and in petitions for your help. In general, Lord, how can I grow closer to you to be in the center of your purpose? Increase my confidence in my faith. I will listen in the quiet of the secret place as I wait for you to speak, in Jesus' name, Amen.

This young, male kingfisher is less colorful than his female siblings. The female has a rust feather band around the belly. Both sexes have the spiky topnotch. This bird is anti-social to the point of being labeled a "loner." Only during the nesting season do they tolerate each other and cooperate as mated pairs. Together they dig a dark tunnel in the earthen bank. The female deposits the eggs and both mom and dad spend time on the nest to incubate and birth their family. After birth, they are nurtured by mom, while dad goes out to hunt down the next meal as his contribution. After only 5 weeks, full-feathered and able to fly, the newest kingfishers leave home forever. In one week they are hunting for their food and beginning the "loner" lifestyle. They do not tolerate or associate with other birds, including their own family members. This brings new meaning to "independence!" One might think there are some insecurity or anger management issues to be worked out before the next mating season. However, they seem to forgive and forget much sooner than we do.

"Do not let any unwholesome talk come out of your mouths, but only what is helpful for building others up according to their needs, that it may benefit those who listen. And do not grieve the Holy Spirit of God, with whom you were sealed for the day of redemption. Get rid of all bitterness, rage and anger, brawling and slander, along with every form of malice. Be kind and compassionate to one another, forgiving each other, just as in Christ God forgave you."

Ephesians 4:29-32

Was there ever a time when you withdrew from family and friends and began the "loner" existence? Maybe it was for a few days or maybe for months or years? Did you feel better or worse about yourself as you made the changes from belonging to isolation? What were the reasons that you withdrew? Did you ever figure that out? If not, did you seek counsel or were you sure you were right about why you didn't fit in? Do you have trouble forgiving others for their mistakes? Has anyone ever had to forgive you for your mistakes? Do you usually want to strike back at someone who has hurt you? These are issues that do not get healed overnight. But God wants to heal every single one! You may want to return to this page a few times when you want more answers from the Lord. He is our Healer, Counselor and our Prince of Peace.

Prayer: Come, Holy Spirit, reveal any unrighteous anger, unforgiveness, malice or wicked ways in me. I need your healing touch and your loving grace to forgive others, forgive myself and to reach out to those I have hurt to ask for their forgiveness. Give me the humility of Christ to admit when I am wrong, to extend grace when others hurt me and to recognize that you, Lord, are the power in me to change. Lord, I need more of you in my life and less of me. In the grace and mercy of Jesus Christ who died to set me free from sin and death, Amen.

PART
2
Lord God, Procreator of All Life on Earth

"**The Lord God formed the man from the dust of the ground and breathed into his nostrils the breath of Life, and the man became a living being. Now the Lord God had planted a garden in the east, in Eden; and there He put the man He had formed. And the Lord God commanded the man, 'You are free to eat from any tree in the garden; but you must not eat from the tree of the knowledge of good and evil, for when you eat of it you will surely die.' The Lord God said, 'It is not good for the man to be alone. I will make a helper suitable for him.'**

"**Then the Lord God made a woman from the rib He had taken out of the man and He brought her to the man. For this reason a man will leave his father and mother and be united to his wife, and they will become one flesh. The man and his wife were both naked and they felt no shame.**"

Genesis 2:7-8, 16-18, 22, 24-25

The tree of the knowledge of good and evil soon became a temptation that the first couple on earth could not resist. They chose their free will and ate the forbidden fruit. "Death" is the result of the sin of disobedience created by free will granted to the human race by God in the very beginning.

So our Lord God has been creating life for thousands of years, both male and female, to procreate the human race and all God's creatures in His Creation. Our world of living creatures in nature is filled with beauty, majesty, power and grace. But when sin entered His perfect Creation, we, human beings, lost fellowship with God and the road to death became our destiny.

Have you faced this truth? Are you a blood-bought child of God with eternity in your future with Jesus? As you read and worship through this devotional, our prayer is that, yes, you have either settled that question, or you will take care to settle it before you finish this book.

"**'Here I am! I stand at the door and knock. If anyone hears my voice and opens the door, I will come in and eat with him, and he with me.'**"

Revelation 3:20

More Love to Thee, O Christ

453

1. More love to thee, O Christ, more love to thee!
2. Once earth-ly joy I craved, sought peace and rest;
3. Let sor-row do its work, come grief and pain;
4. Then shall my lat-est breath whis-per thy praise;

Hear thou the prayer I make on bend-ed knee.
now thee a-lone I seek, give what is best.
sweet are thy mes-sen-gers, sweet their re-frain,
this be the part-ing cry my heart shall raise;

This is my ear-nest plea: More love, O Christ, to thee;
This all my prayer shall be: More love, O Christ, to thee;
when they can sing with me: More love, O Christ, to thee;
this still its prayer shall be: More love, O Christ, to thee;

more love to thee, more love to thee!
more love to thee, more love to thee!
more love to thee, more love to thee!
more love to thee, more love to thee!

WORDS: Elizabeth P. Prentiss, 1869
MUSIC: William H. Doane, 1870

MORE LOVE TO THEE
64.64.66.44

28

In Part 2, enjoy God's plan in nature for procreation. You will see some amazing photos that display God's miraculous plan for birthing new generations. Gaze at this perfect pair of loving birds sharing a tree branch in the sunlight on a warm spring morning. Do you sense the serenity of this scene? Do you feel the gentleness of God's presence as He smiles down on them? Just as God knows what this day has in store for us, He instinctively is leading mom and pop. Maybe they are going to linger together and enjoy some downtime among the trees, or both may fly off in different directions. We will never know, but God knows! Their Creator loves this pair of sweet birds. How much more does He love you, who are made in His image?

"Some Pharisees came to him to test him. They asked, 'Is it lawful for a man to divorce his wife for any and every reason?' 'Haven't you read,' He replied, 'that at the beginning the Creator made them male and female, and said, 'For this reason a man will leave his father and mother and be united to his wife, and the two will become one flesh?' So they are no longer two, but one. Therefore, what God has joined together, let man not separate.'"

Matthew 19:3-6

This scripture is often part of Christian wedding ceremonies. It simply states God's plan for procreation and faithfulness to each other as husband and wife. Back in the Old Testament, God told Abraham that He, God, was going to make him the father of many nations, and so it has come to pass. One generation after another has followed God's plan for populating the world by birthing and raising children and then sending them off to start a new generation. In nature, God has provided the same. He has given us the opportunity to appreciate all the living creatures He has put around us. What are your favorite birds? Do you like to feed the birds? Have you taken photos of your favorites? Let's give thanks for nature.

Prayer: Lord God, how praiseworthy and precious are your bird families in the natural. Thank you for all your variety in the forests and along the roadside. Please help the bluebirds to thrive and be plentiful in the years ahead for the continual display of your beauty. Lord, the earth is full of your glory, and I love to explore, finding the new life you are constantly creating and giving thanks to you for my own new life in Christ, Amen. Now can you sing along with the birds?

"All creatures of our God and King, join now in His praise to sing, Al-le-lu-ia, Al-le-lu-ia, Al-le-lu-ia, (repeat)." God may join you or finish the song with you! He wrote the words!

These calling cranes are most likely announcing, to let others know, that it is mating time. They are well-known for their "tribal war dance" or "wild courtship antics." If you are invited to this performance, you will likely tell others the next day that it was your most memorable sight ever in the avian kingdom. The eggs the female lays are incubated both by mom and pop crane. In 30 to 32 days, these sandhills become parents and look after their young for about a year. You may agree that this photo is stunning, from the long legs reflected in the pools of water to the sunset reflected in the background. God is to be praised!

"As God's fellow workers, we urge you not to receive God's grace in vain. For He says, 'in the time of my favor I heard you, and in the day of salvation I helped you. I tell you, now is the time of God's favor, now is the day of salvation.'"

2 Corinthian 6:1-2

God is calling the cranes to start a new generation, and in their instinctive obedience to call out to each other, we might want to stop and listen to the word of God in 2 Corinthians. Could the calling cranes be reminding us that God often calls out to us? Have you heard God's call for salvation, the unmerited grace to receive forgiveness for your sins? Today is the day of salvation, a free gift from God. Or maybe you are saved but a bit backslidden from close fellowship with Jesus, our Redeemer King? He is a jealous God, and He may be calling you back to safety underneath His wings. He wants intimacy with you in His secret place, your heart! Can you allow God's heart to invade your heart so you can become more like Him?

Prayer: Lord God, forgive me when I take my relationship with you for granted. I am all too often self-centered, busy with what is good, but not with what is BEST! To know you and to hear your voice, Lord, I know I must spend quality time with you. That is how close relationships are formed and blessed. I want to spend time not only talking with you, but also listening and waiting for your answers. Today, I receive your death on the Cross of Calvary as payment for my sin debt. Come, Holy Spirit and fill me with your power to set me free from the bondage I have accepted as life. I desire the best, the new life in Christ and a daily time in your presence that I might hear you and live for you and your purposes. Lord, be glorified in my life, in Jesus' name and for His sake, Amen.

It is thrilling to see the V-formation every fall of the Canada geese heading south. Males and females honk greetings and signals to each other as they travel. The exuberant courtship displays and mating routines of these stately birds still interest nature lovers. Calling out to his mate, he is a fierce defender of her and their offspring. After first giving fair warning, the male begins his "attack dance," and an aroused gander will charge any suspected enemy, even one as large as an elk. Family protection is a gander's number-one priority, so the Canada geese have a reputation of being exemplary parents. They stay with their young for almost 9 months. Some pairs may have as long as 20 years together before disease or a predator changes their togetherness. What a love story! What a Creator God! All praise to Him!

"Some Pharisees came and tested Him by asking, 'Is it lawful for a man to divorce his wife?' 'What did Moses command you?' He replied. They said, 'Moses permitted a man to write a certificate of divorce and send her away.' 'It was because your hearts were hard that Moses wrote you this law,' Jesus replied."

Mark 10:2-5

The difference between bird togetherness and marriage between a man and woman is "Covenant." "For richer or poorer, in sickness and in health, till death we do part." Jesus came to not only soften hardened hearts but to make all sinners' hearts brand new! Describe the condition of your heart to Jesus right now. Do you need to make any adjustments in your heart to be right with God? Use this time to pray your own personal petitions of praise and thanksgiving. Ask for more of the unconditional love of Christ in your marriage or in other daily home and work relationships. Don't forget to spend some time listening to God's voice! When you hear Him, follow with obedience.

Prayer: Lord God, Author of the marriage covenant between a man and a woman, I want more of your love and forgiveness in my daily relationships. Help me never to take others for granted and to always be ready to pray for them, give encouragement, lend a listening ear and walk the extra mile to help them become all you have called them to be. Stop me when my heart grows faint and far from you. I will read your word, practice private worship, spend more time in prayer and/or just get started with a daily prayer time. Come, Holy Spirit. I desire to never miss a word from you, Lord. Listening to you speak to me is my heart's desire, in Jesus' name, Amen.

During the first few weeks, a young loon usually travels on its parent's back. The young leave the nest soon after hatching and then it's off to the water. In 12 weeks, with many meals like the one mom is offering, Louie will be in the air able to fly. To describe the call of the loon is very individual because it touches deep down in the soul of the listener. Some say it sounds like a cry, others like a laugh, even a yodel. With gracious movements, the loon swims and dives deep, often disappearing for some time. They can go as deep as 150 feet looking for a meal.

"'I am the Lord; that is my name! I will not give my glory to another or my praise to idols. See, the former things have taken place, and the new things I declare before they spring into being I announce them to you.'"

Isaiah 42:8-9

Over much of North America, the loon is disappearing. Contamination of lakes by acid rain is possibly a reason, along with oil slicks and the shrinking of the American wilderness. In the book of Isaiah, this scripture is highly regarded as a very important prophetic insight into the coming Messiah, Jesus Christ. God reminds us that He declares these most life-changing events years before they happened, and if we believe Him, we will declare that Jesus is coming again to establish the new heaven and the new earth. It hasn't happened yet, but we believe and we wait for that wonderful day. If the loon in America becomes extinct, will there be loons in heaven? Most certainly they will flourish there. Why? Because Jesus Christ makes all things new. He loves all of His creation, especially this faithful mom and chick. How much greater is His love for you!

Prayer: Lord God, I am bursting with praise as I anticipate my excitement when I see these magnificent loons in heaven. Make a way where there seems to be no way, to make the loons plentiful again in America. You, God, announced your birth long before you were born, and the former practice of forgiveness of sin disappeared when you, Jesus, bled on the cross. You made a way for the entire world to be saved by grace with faith in you. Sometimes when I go deep, Lord, I am overwhelmed by your story of selfless love. You went to hell in my place and then rose victorious over death and appeared alive again on earth. Lord God, I pray today that your miraculous signs and wonders would begin to happen in my city. Many have turned away or have not yet believed. America needs many eyes and hearts to be opened. Lord, your Holy-Spirit power and our prayers are needed to turn this land back to you. I will continue to pray in the words of the Apostle Paul: "Pray without ceasing, in everything give thanks, for this is the will of God for me in Christ Jesus," Amen.

The Caspian is the largest tern in the world. Terns and gulls belong to the same family, and might be expected to borrow an occasional trait from each other. You could say that the Caspian terns impersonate gull-like traits. They are not very social, traveling alone or in small groups. They keep their young in the nest by pecking and beating them until they crouch for shelter. Is this chick abuse? No, this treatment is a safety measure. If the young terns wander out of the nest they will likely be killed or eaten by a predator. A tern can sit in the water while paddling, and fish in that position as well as skimming low over the water to fish. In this photo, notice that mom is ready to receive lunch for her newest chick. Dad should be on his way home with the goodies soon.

"Sing to the Lord a new song, His praise from the ends of the earth, you who go down to the sea, and all that is in it, you islands, and all who live in them."

Isaiah 42:10

Fortunately, as we take a look at the new baby under mom's wing, we notice that there are no signs of pecking going on, nor has there been any beating. But mom does have her little one tucked under her body to keep him still. He sure looks safe doesn't he? Mom's new song is a newborn chick, and God is giving her patience as she waits for dad. This is a picture of a joyous song of protection and tender-loving care. What a good mom!

Prayer: Lord God, thank you for your plan to fill the earth with beautiful life and provision for all. Your timing is always perfect, and your new songs brighten my day. Thank you for rest at night from my labors. May tomorrow be another example of your grace and goodness in my journey to live for you, Lord. Thank you for the family you have given me, and the joy I receive when I am caring for and providing for my family. Lord, listen to your child singing!
"Oh, come let us adore Him, Oh, come let us adore Him, Oh, come let us adore Him,
Christ, the Lord.
For He alone is worthy, for He alone is worthy, for He alone is worthy,
Christ the Lord.
I'll praise His name forever, I'll praise His name forever, I'll praise His name forever,
Christ the Lord," Amen.

CASPIAN TERN – *dad with lunch*   *Sterna caspia*

New Jersey   *Uncommon*

....

This largest tern in the world resembles a large gull. His stout, reddish bill with a small dark mark near the tip sets the Caspian apart from all other terns. They prefer inland areas. So gull-like, he could be called an impersonator! The Caspian has two different positions when flying. If fishing near the water, he flaps his wings continuously with his bill pointed down very near the water where he hopes to find his next meal. During a long flight, he flies high above other birds, bill pointed straight ahead, wings held wide and still. He soars on the currents like a gull. He's been known to steal food from other birds and their nests. The Caspian is the least social of all terns, traveling alone or in small groups. Does stealing food from others have anything to do with his isolation? Only God knows!

"Meanwhile His disciples urged Him, 'Rabbi, eat something.' But He said to them, 'I have food to eat that you know nothing about.' Then His disciples said to each other, 'Could someone have brought Him food?' 'My food,' said Jesus, 'is to do the will of Him who sent me and to finish His work.'"

John 4:31-34

Doing the will of His Father in heaven was the number-one priority for Jesus. There was nothing more important than enduring the upcoming humiliation on the cross for the salvation of those whom He created in His image. Remember when, at 12 years old, He went to the temple without His parents knowing where He was. They were upset with Him but he said to them, "Don't you know I have to be about my Father's business?" Food was secondary for Jesus. First was hearing the voice of His Father, and then obeying no matter how hungry he was. The disciples' number-one priority was food for the stomach. We are like that! Heaven forbid, we should miss a meal! But the truth is, we may be spiritually hungry, and instead of going to God for spiritual food, we turn to drink, food, drugs or other distractions, thinking that they will satisfy our emptiness. God and only God can satisfy our emptiness! In the photo, dad is returning to the nest with a delightful treat for mom and their chick. If God provides for the tiny chicks, think how much more He will provide for you, His child!

Prayer: Lord God, help me with my daily priorities. Teach me how to start my day with "taste and see that the Lord is good." I want to be nourished by God's word and make it a daily habit. I want to be like Jesus who always heard His Father's voice and wanted to be about His Father's business. Lord, your business is my business. Without you I can do nothing. I will draw close to you so you will draw close to me. Help me make my number-one priority today to join you in your plan for me and glorify you in what we are doing together. I will continually give you praise with thanksgiving for what you are accomplishing here on earth and in my life. I am so grateful for your unfailing love, Amen.

The next two photos make up a black skimmer family. Here is mom and her chicks. The black skimmer is a gull-like bird. Most unusual is the fact that both male and female have the exact same coloring. Their bills are unusual and exactly alike. The bottom bill grows longer than the top, which is only half as long. God created them this way to help in grabbing fish out of the water and securing it for the ride home to the nest. Mom sits here in the sandy nest overseeing and protecting the newborns. Today dad is bringing home "take-out" because they are too young to leave the nest.

"He (Jesus) is the image of the invisible God, the first born over all creation. For by Him all things were created: things in heaven and on earth, visible and invisible, whether thrones or powers or rulers or authorities; all things were created by Him and for Him. He is before all things, and in Him all things hold together."

Colossians 1:15-17

The family – mom, dad and offspring – is God's creative plan for filling the earth with goodness and grace. Raising a family in a fallen world is not an easy task, but none of us who have children and grandchildren would want it any other way. God is still holding everything together with His powerful word, and we continue to be blessed, day after day, by our families. An attitude of gratitude is in order! If you belong to Jesus, you also belong to the family of God here on earth, and will enter heaven and live forever with all of God's family. Thanks be to God, our Heavenly Father!

Prayer: Lord God, there are no words to express my gratitude for your amazing grace and protection that has brought me through thick and thin, storms and pain, hurts and bad habits, graduations, weddings, new babies, anniversaries, sad deaths and frustrating circumstances. Through it all, you and your loving presence has brought comfort, healing and hope. Your love never fails! Lord, protect my family today from the evil one as you continue to hold your creation together with your powerful word. I, your humble child, give you highest praise and lift up on high the name of Jesus, my Rock and my Redeemer. Please save all my family, write their names in the book of life so they will be filled with hope for tomorrow, Amen.

In this second skimmer photo, we see dad searching for the "take-out" meal to bring back to the nest to make the young babies happy. Dad has a magnificent wingspan and is lowering down to skim the water's edge. He perseveres until he has secured a fish good and tight between his uneven bills. He is almost always successful, and his tiny children grow and flourish because both parents take responsibility for the welfare of their beautiful family. After the babies are bigger and can leave the nest, they may all go out together to hunt. Mom and dad often take this time to settle down, half-buried in the sand for a snooze or to hide their heads under their neck feathers. After all, us parents need our rest and quiet time!

"And He is the head of the body, the church; He is the beginning and the firstborn from among the dead, so that in everything He might have the supremacy. For God was pleased to have all His fullness dwell in Him, and through Him to reconcile to Himself all things, whether things on earth or things in heaven, by making peace through His blood, shed on the cross."

Colossians 1:18-20

How close to nature's ways has God created our ways. Wisdom and knowledge are ours if we are willing to pursue them. The first wisdom and/or knowledge that we need is the account of the life of Jesus Christ as revealed in the Holy Bible. He is alive in every book, including both the Old and New testaments. Jesus Christ is the Supreme One, having supremacy over everything. Older folks need to tell the younger generation of their life experiences with our Supreme God. In the last book, Revelation, God says, "We are saved by the blood of the Lamb and the word of our testimony." Testimonies are to be given, passed on, cherished and honoring to God, as we tell our story everywhere we go. Leave an account of the amazing grace of God for those you leave behind.

Prayer: Lord God, thank you that I have a testimony to share with the world. As a Disciple of Christ, I will never get tired of talking about you, Jesus, and never stop talking to you, God, with a grateful heart. I'll keep singing hymns and songs to glorify you and pronounce your supremacy to the world you created. Oh, that everyone would know you, Jesus, and live for you. I love You, Lord, and enjoy this time I spend in your beautiful presence. I'll be back to sing again tomorrow, in Jesus' name, Amen.

These snow geese breed in the Arctic regions of Siberia and North America. Do not confuse the flight formation of the snow geese with the flight formation for the Canada geese. Snow geese = U, Canada geese = V. This snow geese U-shaped flight formation is usually at altitudes of around 1,000 feet! This photo is most inspiring, not just for the serenity of the scene, but also for the togetherness of the family. Mom, dad and junior gliding slowly forward, all eyes fixed upon the future spaces, so contented on this slow-paced journey. No hurry, no worry, just each other and the wilderness to enjoy. If a title could be placed on this photo, it might be "Inner Peace." Also note the amazing reflections on the water. Perfect lighting, with unique surroundings and wings pinned back to show off size and stature. Bravo, man with camera! Peace!

"Peace I leave with you; my peace I give you. I do not give to you as the world gives. Do not let your hearts be troubled and do not be afraid."

John 14:27

Jesus is reassuring His disciples that even though He is going to leave them soon they should not be worried or concerned, because He will send the Holy Spirit to be in them to bring them His peace. He also said that it is the peace that passes all understanding. It is an amazing gift from God's heart to ours and if you want it, just ask Jesus for a fresh infilling of His Spirit. He is waiting for you to ask. He wants all of His followers to be filled daily with His Spirit. Fear, frustration, tiredness, anger and sadness are conditions that rob us of our peace. God's perfect love casts out all fear, and we receive His love through the powerful Holy Spirit. He gives to those who ask! We have not because we ask not. Let's ask Him now:

Prayer: Come, Holy Spirit and fill me up afresh. Bring peace, joy and the love of my God to my weary heart as I sit in the quiet to worship. Lord, I want to receive more of your unconditional love and I choose now to spend the next few minutes in worship and listening to you speak to me. I am still and I know that you are God. I remember that you want me to sit and linger with you often so I don't miss a single blessing. Thank you for placing me in the family of God, in Jesus' name, Amen.

PART
3
LORD God, Provider for Life on Earth

"Then God said, 'Let the land produce vegetation: seed bearing plants and trees on the land that bear fruit with seed in it, according to their various kinds.' And it was so. And there was evening and there was morning – the third day."

Genesis 1:11, 13

Due to sinful mankind and our disrespect for who God is, He flooded the earth after Noah built the now-famous ark. When the flood receded and man once again inhabited the land, God made a covenant with man. He made a promise to never flood the earth again, and He fulfilled the promise with a rainbow in the sky. Today we still look for the rainbow as a sign of God's faithfulness to us.

Moving on to the New Testament, we know that many, many years passed by with no words from God after the end of Malachi. Rebellion among God's people in His creation caused His silence until the Gospels of Matthew, Mark, Luke and John. Enter Mary, Joseph, and the Christ Child. We all know and love the Christmas Story and always look forward to that Celebration every Dec. 25.

At age 30, Jesus begins His ministry by choosing 12 disciples. That one solitary life changed the world forever. Jesus was crucified and suffered a brutal, agonizing death, but he rose from the dead and is seated in heaven waiting for us to join him in life everlasting. Not only do we have our physical needs taken care of by God, but now we have our spiritual needs met in Jesus Christ, our Savior, from sin and death. It is our greatest decision in life to make Jesus our Lord and our Best Friend.

Part 3 represents God's provision for our everyday needs of food, water, shelter, and most importantly, our spiritual needs. God has an eternal plan for saving a sinful world and to bring us hope. The hope of the world was born on the first Christmas well over 2,000 years ago. He went to the cross at age 33 after ministering among us for three years. He was born fully man and fully God so we can get to know and love Him while we are here.

"For God so loved the world that he gave us His one and only Son, that whoever believes in Him shall not perish but have eternal life. For God did not send His Son into the world to condemn the world, but to save the world through Him."

John 3:16-17

314 In the Garden
(I Come to the Garden Alone)

1. I come to the gar-den a-lone while the dew is still on the ros-es, and the voice I hear fall-ing on my ear, the Son of God dis-clos-es.

2. He speaks, and the sound of his voice is so sweet the birds hush their sing-ing, and the mel-o-dy that he gave to me with-in my heart is ring-ing.

3. I'd stay in the gar-den with him though the night a-round me be fall-ing, but he bids me go; thru the voice of woe his voice to me is call-ing.

Refrain

And he walks with me, and he talks with me, and he tells me I am his own; and the joy we share as we tar-ry there, none oth-er has ev-er known.

WORDS: C. Austin Miles, 1913 (Jn. 20:11-18)
MUSIC: C. Austin Miles, 1913; adapt. by Charles H. Webb, 1987

GARDEN
89.557 with Refrain

The American pelican has several attributes that relate to the human race. Some humans love to fish, and many are "Master Fishermen," winning prizes for their large catches. This pelican is a Master Fisher for starters. Second, he has a good work ethic and favorable family values. Third, even though on land he is awkward looking, with an oversized bill and feet, he is handsome and serene while in flight. Perhaps you have heard this jingle before: "A wonderful bird is the pelican, his bill holds more than his belli-can!" It is hard to believe that his bill holds almost 3 gallons of water! Another phenomenon: The parents will fly 100 or more miles to find food to bring back to their young in the nest. They prefer fish as their life-sustaining food along with all that water.

"Jesus answered (the woman at the well), 'Everyone who drinks this water will be thirsty again, but whoever drinks the water I give him will never thrist. Indeed, the water I give him will become in him a spring of water welling up to eternal life.'"

John 4:13-14

Growing up and playing with siblings near a creek, named "Mud Creek," we had a chant when we were thirsty: "Water, water everywhere and not a drop to drink." When we got back home, we were blessed to have well water to quench our thirst. This should remind us all that in many third world countries there is very little clean water to sustain life. There are great ministries that not only drill wells in these impoverished countries, but also bring the Gospel of Christ to give residents Living Water that wells up to eternal life. These are worthy ministries to support if God lays it on your heart to do so. The Living Water that Jesus gives is His Holy Spirit alive in us. If you have it and keep filled with it, you will never be spiritually thirsty again. The pelican carries a lot of water in his bill; so let that remind us to ask Jesus Christ for a fresh infilling of His Living Water each day.

Prayer: Come, Holy Spirit and help me be the hands and feet of Jesus today. Who needs Living Water that will well up to eternal life? Give me boldness to speak the truth in love to whosoever does not know Jesus. Give me ears to listen, hear and understand what their needs are. Help me share with them where they can find Living Water to quench their thirst. In you, Lord, is the deepest well in all creation. You will never run out of the pure water that wells up to eternal life. In Jesus' name, Amen.

When this heron returns to the nest with his awesome treasure, there is sure to be a riot. The young, once they see what dad is hauling into the nest, will push, shove and squeal like hungry piglets. An unbalanced young bird will flail out of control, flapping wings to rebalance himself. The last thing he wants to do is fall out of the nest. It is a long way down to the ground. Can you just imagine the noise going on up there at the top of that tree? Young bills stab and wrestle morsels from the parent's bill. If you are under that tree, you will be ducking the debris from a massive food fight! Hard hats are recommended when standing below on the ground. Dad does not find this gourmet treat every day, so to describe this scene as joyous is an understatement.

"In that day, sing about a fruitful vineyard: I, the Lord, watch over it; I water it continually; I guard it day and night so that no one may harm it."

Isaiah 27:2-3

Think back to a time long ago, or maybe just yesterday, when the joy and excitement was overpowering in the room you were sharing with others. Maybe it was a graduation, wedding or the birth of a child. Perhaps you have been in the room when God answered a prayer with a miracle! There are many times when God has filled us with great joy and thanksgiving. Can you also visualize the elation in the nest of the very young great blue herons? Yes, God is full of surprises and we are amazed at His many miracles and His goodness to us. Excitement controlled the whole small town when my mother gave birth to my twin brothers! We were a family with three daughters. My father was the most joy-filled of all as he stopped on the way home and bought a second crib. The joy never once left his face. That was 65 years ago: One heartbeat, no ultrasound, no advanced warning or preparation. It's the same for the heron world, no dream or knowledge that dad is flying home with caviar!

Prayer: Lord God, the forest and all that is in it testifies to your glory, and your bountiful, breathtaking creation is forever. You are faithful to provide for my every need and much more. My gratitude overflows because I am made in your image and you granted me great value in your Kingdom here on earth. I intend to continue to sing your praises over and over forever. I am so glad that you watch over me just like you do for the heron and the sparrow. I know they are singing with me because they are happy, too. Let the Redeemed of the Lord say so! In the precious and glorious name of Jesus, my loving Redeemer, my Fruitful Vine, Amen.

Practicing patience is a winning natural trait of this heron. On the next page of this book is another photo of this same greenback. When you see it you will know why there are two photos of the bird situated in this part of the devotional. This heron knows that good things come to those who wait! When hunting, he is known for his quiet, motionless, patient techniques. The only things that move when looking for his next meal are his eyes. The green heron's ability to transform into a lifeless, log-like object helps lure one breakfast after another into his hungry, squatty body. Running fast to catch something is out of the question with such short legs. Patience is a virtue and he has mastered that!

"I waited patiently for the Lord; He turned to me and heard my cry. He lifted me out of the slimy pit, out of the mud and mire; He set my feet on a rock and gave me a firm place to stand."

Psalm 40:1-2

Are you working on mastering patience, or is the lack of patience mastering you? Sometimes lack of patience fosters anger and frustration. Both of those emotions can be unhealthy for our bodies if we don't keep them in check. If left unchecked, we can hurt people emotionally and physically. Our own healing is so important to concentrate on in these situations. It is common knowledge that "hurting people hurt people," or another way to say the same thing is "wounded people wound people." Jesus Christ is the greatest Healer alive through the power of the Holy Spirit alive in us. If you do not know Jesus, it is imperative that you get to know Him personally and allow Him to become your Best Friend here on earth. We get to know Him by spending quality time with Him, just like we do with our own families. Worship and prayer are needed elements to foster God's healing in us. Worship and pray alone and with others as often as possible. Receive His healing love daily. Healing happens when you are alone with God and when God is in the midst of you and others. Neglecting church prayer meetings, healing prayer ministry meetings and worship times lets God know all about your unbelief. Try cooperating with God and see what happens! He has patiently waited for you for a very long time. It's your move, Friend!

Prayer: Lord God, Healer of all emotional, physical and spiritual pain and Healer of my unspoken needs, minister to me now in the places where I hurt. Show me where I need to forgive, where I need to make amends and where I can show your much needed love, grace and mercy. Please help me stop the cycle of sin that hurts others and myself. I need more of your healing power in my life. I'll talk to you again very soon, in the name of Jesus, who gave His life that I might be healed, Amen.

Not only is the green-backed heron patient, but so is the photographer. He had to persevere for a lengthy time to capture both of these photos in God's timing. It was very important for this camera to be motionless, keeping an eye-on-the-prize for the outcome he wanted. Another bravo, for not only marvelous success but how about the quality of the color, the clarity of the photo and the ability to see the reward in the mouth of Mr. Patient! Two patient men at one event: How rare is that? Just kidding, LOL!

"He put a new song in my mouth, a hymn of praise to our God, many will see and fear and put their trust in the Lord."

Psalm 40:3

God has a sense of humor, and as a Christian it helps to see the lighter side of situations now and then. There is a new song stirring in this author's heart as the writing progresses. It has been a very enjoyable task and I will write more after this is done. So going back to the patience of the green-backed heron, both the photographer and author of this book know a little bit about patience. We both taught our entire careers in an elementary public school! The scripture above says that because of our new songs of praise, many will put their trust in the Lord. That is what this devotional is, and that has been our prayer throughout this new journey. Is your patience fragile? Do you sometimes yell at your family when you really wish you had the peace of God that passes all understanding? Talk to Jesus about it. He not only understands, but He is the Prince of Peace and He will help you get there. God's answers are always just one prayer away!

Prayer: Thank you from the bottom of my heart, Lord, for all of nature that teaches me so much about myself and how to become more like you as I continue in this intimate relationship. This meditation time has been interesting and also restorative. I love listening to you as I fill my heart with your words from the bible. As I trust in you, I am ready to walk with you today to wherever you lead. I choose to look for you more in nature instead of always being in a hurry to get somewhere. Now I will sit back, close my eyes and listen for your voice because I love you, Lord, and desperately need to hear you again. In Jesus' name and for His glory, Amen.

Amazing instincts bless the herring gull. This crab is probably being let go from his bill to land on hard ground. It will crack open when it hits the pavement and "Herry" will swoop down and retrieve it in his bill and fly away home. These gulls doze lazily around the shore for a meal to be flung onto the beach by a heavy wave. Can you then picture the scramble to be the first to take flight with the newest deposit from the sea? It brings new meaning to "Fresh Seafood Market!" A phenomenon: This gull, a strong, forward flier, can hover forward or backward with hardly a flick of his wings. This photo shows "Hovering Herry" dropping the crab to break the shell. Back at the nest, the young herring gulls peck at the red spot on the parent's bill to make it regurgitate the food and share another successful trip to the shore.

"The earth is the Lord's and everything in it, the world and all who live in it, for He founded it upon the seas, and established it upon the waters."

Psalm 24:1-2

Visualize the frenzied scene on shore waiting for the next big wave to wash up a treasure. Are you reminded, just a little, about "Black Friday" at the mall? Yes, we are prone to get excited about things that do not excite God; distractions that the world provides because everybody is doing that today! If God is our one and only attraction, then each day we will want to put Him first. We can do this by reading His word, spending time in His presence, giving thanks and praise because we love Him, and finding His will for the new day before us and seeking His peace. Not as the world gives, but the peace that passes all understanding. His peace is the peace that satisfies and quiets the heart. This is a free gift for all believers who surrender daily. Another free gift is joy! What brings you the joy of the Lord today?

Prayer: Lord God, I confess that many days I do not make you my number-one priority. Help me, in my daily time with you, to be filled with the Holy Spirit. I need to make more time for worship, prayer and praise. I am desperate to experience more of your manifest presence. My desire is to change my selfish habit into the very best habit. I will remember that in your presence is the fullness of joy, and your joy is the strength that I need to live a surrendered life for you. Everything good in my life comes from you. I know that I rarely thank you for all your goodness to me. You are so patient with me, more than I deserve. It feels good to do this confessing to you. I know I am already forgiven, but I never want to take you for granted because you mean too much to me. In the loving, forgiving name of Jesus, the Son of God, Creator of everything good, Amen.

The adult roseate spoonbill, when mature, has a spoon-shaped bill. The odd bill is used to strain food items out of water. His bright pinkish-rose coloring leads many Florida tourists to think they have seen a flamingo. In this photo, "Billy" is taking a few minutes out of his busy day to do some preening. Selecting some troublesome, old feathers that have lost their purpose and color, he plucks them out and discards them. God does the same thing with us when a bad habit needs to be eliminated and replaced with a healthier one. God calls it sanctification through the power of the Holy Spirit alive in us. We feel so much better when we cooperate with God in this process. When we are changing to be more like Jesus, He is glorified and we are being sanctified.

"If we confess our sins, He is faithful and just and will forgive us our sins and purify us from all unrighteousness."

1 John 1:9

Have you ever gained too much weight on a vacation trip and then struggled to get back to a healthier weight when back home? Maybe you got a ticket for exceeding the speed limit in your car? Or maybe you have spent time gossiping about a neighbor or church member and realized that sin separates us from God. Confession and repentance is the only way back into fellowship with Him. So don't put the treadmill on eBay or try to sell it at a garage sale. Dust it off and get on it for 10 minutes to start, and then work up to 30 minutes by the end of the month. Today is the day to start preening! All things are possible with God. Our obedience shows God our love for Him.

Prayer: Lord God, thank you for the example of preening to remind me that you desire my sanctification. When I knowingly sin, I will confess and repent to keep the needed changes in my character moving into a likeness of you, Jesus Christ, my Lord and Savior. I want to be holy as you are holy! The cross has made it all possible, and I am forever grateful to you, Lord, for shedding your blood to set me free from sin and death. I know that I need daily preening, because I have areas where I need to change how I live, speak and act. You are my only hope for change, Lord, and I am in love with you, my Holy God, in Jesus' name, Amen.

62 All Creatures of Our God and King

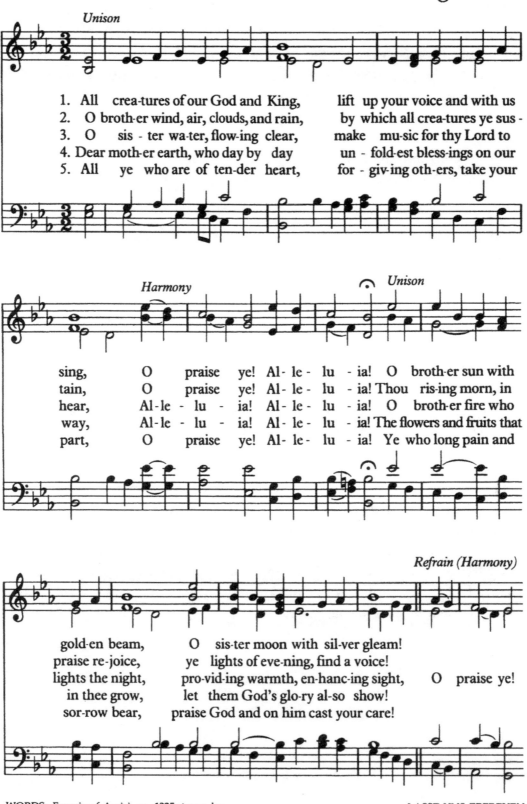

Unison

1. All crea-tures of our God and King, lift up your voice and with us
2. O broth-er wind, air, clouds, and rain, by which all crea-tures ye sus -
3. O sis - ter wa-ter, flow-ing clear, make mu-sic for thy Lord to
4. Dear moth-er earth, who day by day un - fold-est bless-ings on our
5. All ye who are of ten-der heart, for - giv-ing oth-ers, take your

Harmony   *Unison*

sing,   O praise ye! Al- le - lu - ia! O broth-er sun with
tain,   O praise ye! Al- le - lu - ia! Thou ris-ing morn, in
hear,   Al-le - lu - ia! Al- le - lu - ia! O broth-er fire who
way,   Al-le - lu - ia! Al- le - lu - ia! The flowers and fruits that
part,   O praise ye! Al- le - lu - ia! Ye who long pain and

Refrain (Harmony)

gold-en beam,   O sis-ter moon with sil-ver gleam!
praise re-joice,   ye lights of eve-ning, find a voice!
lights the night,   pro-vid-ing warmth, en-hanc-ing sight,   O praise ye!
in thee grow,   let them God's glo-ry al-so show!
sor-row bear,   praise God and on him cast your care!

WORDS: Francis of Assisi, ca. 1225; trans. by
   William H. Draper, 1925, adapt. 1987
MUSIC: *Geistliche Kirchengesänge*, 1623; harm. by Ralph Vaughan Williams, 1906

LASST UNS ERFREUEN
88.44.88 with Refrain

Adapt. © 1989 The United Methodist Publishing House

Unison

O praise ye! Al-le - lu - ia! Al-le - lu - ia! Al-le - lu - ia!

6. And thou, our sister, gentle death,
   waiting to hush our latest breath,
   Alleluia! Alleluia!
   Thou leadest home the child of God,
   and Christ our Lord the way has trod,
   Refrain

7. Let all things their Creator bless,
   and worship him in humbleness,
   O praise ye! Alleluia!
   Praise, praise the Father, praise the Son,
   and praise the Spirit, Three in One!
   Refrain

Blessed Be the Name 63

Bless-ed be the name! Bless-ed be the name! Bless-ed be the name of the Lord! Bless - ed be the name! Bless-ed be the name! Bless-ed be the name of the Lord!

WORDS: USA campmeeting chorus (Ps. 72:19)
MUSIC: USA campmeeting melody; arr. by Ralph E. Hudson, 1887

BLESSED BE THE NAME
Irr.

357 Just as I Am, Without One Plea

1. Just as I am, without one plea,
2. Just as I am, and waiting not
3. Just as I am, though tossed about
4. Just as I am, poor, wretched, blind;
5. Just as I am, thou wilt receive,
6. Just as I am, thy love unknown

but that thy blood was shed for me,
to rid my soul of one dark blot,
with many a conflict, many a doubt,
sight, riches, healing of the mind,
wilt welcome, pardon, cleanse, relieve;
hath broken every barrier down;

and that thou bidst me come to thee,
to thee whose blood can cleanse each spot,
fightings and fears within, without,
yea, all I need in thee to find,
because thy promise I believe,
now, to be thine, yea, thine alone,

Refrain

O Lamb of God, I come, I come.

WORDS: Charlotte Elliott, 1835
MUSIC: William B. Bradbury, 1849

WOODWORTH
LM

63

PHOTOGRAPHER
J. Michael Fuller

Mike holds bachelor's and master's degrees from Albany State University in Albany, NY. He spent 28 years as a 5th and 6th grade teacher, specializing in science. Many students in the Scotia-Glenville School District, Scotia, New York, benefitted from Mike's expertise in teaching about the world around us, above us and beyond. He passed on to his students a love for learning, a respect for each other and a respect for God's creation. Mike and his wife also taught Sunday school for many years before she passed away several years ago.

In retirement, Mike continues his long-time passion for photography. He has been published on "Ranger Rick" and "Audubon" covers, Sierra Club and Audubon Society calendars, and published in "International Wildlife" and other publications. He travels extensively in pursuit of new close-up shots of God's magnificent creatures. He lives in Duanesburg, NY, on his 42-acre farm with pond, woods and hills to climb. His woods are full of songbirds, maybe because he has delicious bird feeders scattered strategically around his quiet property. Mike continues to use his photography ministry to bless others and now to bless those who read "His Eye is on the Sparrow." Mike is passionate about the out-of-doors and enjoys working on the farm when not on the road with his camera.

AUTHOR
Shirley D. Andrews

Shirley is a graduate of Eastman School of Music in Rochester, NY, and has a master's degree from Crane School of Music in Potsdam, NY. She taught elementary public school music for 31 years. Most of those years were in the Scotia-Glenville School District. She also taught music education classes at Schenectady County Community College. Shirley enjoyed her career in teaching and now enjoys leading the Wesley Choir in hymn sings at the Embury Apartments at the Wesley Community in Saratoga Springs, NY. She has two children and two grandchildren.

After retirement and the death of her husband, Shirley pursued a second career as a Certified Lay Minister in the Adirondack District of the United Methodist Church (UMC). She has held leadership positions at Porter Corners UMC, Ballston Spa UMC and led worship at Woodlawn Commons Enriched Living in the Wesley Community in Saratoga Springs. Her passions include writing worship songs and leading worship and small group bible studies. She now has added a new passion for inspirational writing. This is her first attempt at writing devotional books.

REFERENCES

Book of North American Birds, The Reader's Digest Association, Inc. Pleasantville, NY/Montreal - 1990

Peterson Field Guide to Birds of Eastern and Central North America, by Roger Tory Peterson; text copyright 2010 by the Marital Trust B – sixth edition

National Audubon Society Field Guide to North American Birds – Eastern Region; copyright 1994 by Chanticleer Press, Inc. - second edition

www.nationalgeographics.com/mammals/animals

Songbirds and Waterfowl, by H.E. Parkhurst – 1897, New York, Charles Scribner's Sons.

Birds that Hunt and are Hunted – Life Histories of One Hundred and Seventy Birds of Prey, Game Birds and Water Fowl, by Neltje Blanchan – 1898, Doubleday and McClure Co., New York

Holy Bible – NIV- Copyright 1990 – Zondervan Publishing House, Grand Rapids, Michigan

Zondervan Exhaustive Concordance – 1999, Zondervan Publishing House, Grand Rapids, Michigan – second edition

The United Methodist Hymnal, Keyboard Edition – Copyright 1989 The United Methodist Publishing House, Tenth Printing – 2013

The Faith We Sing – United Methodist Song Book – Accompaniment Edition- song on pg. 2146, "His Eye is on the Sparrow," copyright 2000 by Abingdon Press. "His Eye is on the Sparrow," song written in 1905 by Civilla D. Martin and Charles H. Gabriel, 1905 date as recorded in "Then Sings My Soul," by Robert J. Morgan on page 261, 2011. Published in Nashville, Tennessee, by W Publishing, an imprint of Thomas Nelson.

COMING IN EARLY 2018

ANOTHER DEVOTIOANL INSPIRED BY NATURE
"HIS EYE IS ON THE SPARROW" – VOLUME II
AUTHOR – Shirley D. Andrews   PHOTOGRAPHER- J. Michael Fuller

Volume II includes Part 4, which focuses on why we need God's protection. Part 5 is God's plan for eternal life with Jesus for all believers. Believers love God with all their hearts, with all their souls and with all their minds. Jesus calls this the "Greatest Commandment."

Another very important verse is found at the end of the Gospel of Matthew. Jesus calls this one the "Great Commission." He says, "All authority in heaven and on earth has been given to me. Therefore go and make disciples of all nations, baptizing them in the name of the Father and of the Son and of the Holy Spirit, and teaching them to obey everything I have commanded you. And surely I am with you always, to the very end of the age.

ALSO AVAIALBE IN 2018

"THOUGH HE DIED YOUNG, YET HE SPEAKS"
by Shirley D. Andrews

Generations of faith, hope and prayer have its beginnings in the late 1700s with Rev. Zadok Hunn. A graduate of Yale University, he rides horseback on dusty, rutty and sometimes muddy trails, rain or shine, preaching the Gospel of Jesus Christ. Pastor Zadock, filled with the Holy Spirit, gallops from small town to small town, tirelessly spreading the "Good News." Before he dies at age 59, he and his family of followers have planted nine Congregational churches in these towns in Western New York state. Seven of those churches are still open and worshipping God in 2018.

His legacy is now being sustained in his family today, several generations later through this memoir. How grateful the family is for his faith, passion, courage, selflessness and his love for Jesus Christ, our Lord. Someday we will see him in heaven to thank him in person. This story may draw you closer to God and may give you more daily purpose. Or, just maybe, God will send you back to a bible-believing, teaching and praying church!

To God be the Glory Forever and Ever, Amen

Printed in the United States
By Bookmasters